the millennial
Homeowner

A GUIDE TO SUCCESSFULLY
NAVIGATING YOUR FIRST HOME PURCHASE

BY **LAUREN BOWLING**

ISBN: 0997952725
ISBN-13: 978-0997952728

For my brother, who helped me make lemonade out of lemons during my first home purchase.

CONTENTS

INTRODUCTION

If you're a long-time reader of my blog, *L Bee and the Money Tree*, then you know the basic gist of my home-ownership story: I bought my first home at age twenty-six, making less than $40,000 dollars per year, and I only paid $1,800 at closing. (More on how I swung that later.)

It was 2013 when I started looking for my first home, and I was home shopping with my then fiancé. We kept the transaction financially separate—I was on the mortgage, but he had final input on what we bought, which ended up being a foreclosure and complete gut job. He wanted a ton of space, and since I'm a money nerd, I wanted to grow my money via the equity in the home. I was excited about becoming a homeowner, but only reluctantly on board with the property we chose.

Everyone's homebuying journey is different, but mine was particularly terrible. What I didn't expect was how difficult and stressful every aspect of the home buying process would be. Part of it was my own naiveté and biting off more than I could chew by purchasing a fixer-upper, but each step, from finding an agent to getting under contract, seemed fraught with difficulties.

Three months after we closed on our home, I ended up losing thousands of dollars and draining my savings to finish a renovation project because my contractor was doing cheap work and skimming off the top. You'd think as a personal finance blogger I would have known better, but just like with personal finance, school doesn't have a class on how to become a knowledgeable homeowner.

The one thing missing from my story was a trusted resource in the form of someone who had been through the process before. My parents were around, but they'd bought a home decades earlier, and their information and advice were a little outdated in the digital age. I didn't have anywhere to go or anyone to turn to for advice on what I should do when buying a home, from preparing for it financially, to getting through closing, to finally moving into the home itself.

So, why attempt homeownership? After all, don't hip and trendy millennials thrive on being unencumbered and without responsibility?

Well, yes. But even I can admit there was a massive part of me that wanted to own something, to prove that I was capable, sturdy, and smart—the type of person who was responsible and mature enough to own a home. Even at twenty-six, I wanted my own piece of the American Dream: The man, the house, the dog, and the job.

Despite the difficulty, and the thousands of dollars in mistakes that I made along the way, owning a home has turned out to be one of the best decisions I've made for myself. It's allowed me to stabilize my wealth, grow my savings, make passive income from renters, and keep my living expenses low enough to leave my full-time job and pursue my dreams. Those are just the tangible benefits. I've also learned some sweet DIY skills, and pushed myself further both emotionally and physically than I ever thought possible.

But even if you want to buy, many millennials are having a difficult time making their dreams of homeownership a reality.

Why Millennials Aren't Buying Homes

Millennial. Millennial. Millennial. It rolls around in the mouth, doesn't it? One could argue that it is one of the buzziest buzzwords of the last five years. Pick up any print publication or browse a popular news site on any particular day and you'll find at least one article about millennials: How we're the reason workplaces are changing; how we're the most financially savvy generation since the recession, but also the most behind when it comes to earnings, savings, and retirement; and, oh yeah, how we're not buying homes.

Yet for all the positive and negative buzz about millennials, companies are desperately trying to figure out how to market to us. They're building products and brands with social awareness in mind, and writing scores of literature about how to best manage millennials in the workplace. They do this because we're a massive section of the population. In fact, a White House Council of Economic Advisers study reports that over one-third of the population are millennials. Eventually, we'll emerge from our perceived extended adolescence into true adulthood. We'll start running companies, redefining the way global economies work, and, finally, buying real estate.

But the reason millennials haven't purchased homes or stepped in to "save" the flagging economy with our shopping habits and investment accounts is because, at first, we couldn't—47% of millennials have college degrees, more than any other generation in history, but with this highly educated population comes nearly $1 trillion in student loan debt. Add the loan burden to the economic hardship faced by millennials who graduated college during the recession years, and you have a generation stunted by unemployment. Collectively we've lost millions of salary dollars during those high-earning "pre-children" years.

With that kind of math, it's no surprise that millennials are delaying economic milestones like homeownership, marriage, and yes, even children.

This information isn't much of a surprise to anyone, as millennial trends have been well covered in the news. What is surprising to learn, however, is despite the buzz, a large knowledge gap still exists, particularly when it comes to reaching those economic milestones previously mentioned. I'm talking specifically about making the biggest— and potentially most expensive—purchase of your lifetime: A home to call your own.

....

Buying a house today has completely different implications than it did even ten years ago, and while the waters ahead of us aren't uncharted, they are, for the most part, foreign to the average millennial.

....

Looking back on my experience of buying, renovating, and investing in my first home, I began to wonder: If I had a better idea of what lay before me, would I have made better decisions? *Absolutely.* Would it have kept me from feeling so overwhelmed and alone? *Undoubtedly.*

So I wrote this book to make the road to homeownership better and easier to understand. Hopefully after reading it you'll feel both prepared and empowered to take your first steps into homeownership!

CHAPTER 1

Am I Really Ready to Own?

Before we can talk about emotionally and financially preparing for homeownership, we first need to discern if homeownership makes sense for you. Some readers may be on the fence, while others may desire to buy a home even when it's not the best financial option. This chapter covers ground for everyone, no matter what situation you're in!

The words "homeownership" and "American Dream" often go together, and for good reason. The benefits of becoming a homeowner are widely known: financial stability, tax benefits, and the pride of being able to say, "This is mine."

But what about when homeownership isn't a good move? Since 2009, homeownership rates have fallen to less than 35% for those under the age of thirty-five, mostly because of crippling student loan debt and a generational penchant for freedom, flexibility, and keeping cash in the bank. In the last few years, young Americans have realized that homeownership isn't necessarily a one-size-fits-all exercise.

If you're someone who is contemplating homeownership, here are a few compelling reasons to put it off.

You're Not in Love With Your Location

Feeling trapped by your one-year lease? Wait until you sign away a big chunk of your nest egg for a thirty-year mortgage. Sure, houses can be bought and sold, so you're not completely tied down, but with taxes, closing costs, and interest, the rule of thumb is that it can take up to five years to recoup your money on a home purchase. This is why financial experts near and far recommend only buying a home if you're looking to put down roots in that specific location for the next five to seven years.

It Doesn't Make Sense for You Financially

In many metro areas, such as New York City and San Francisco, it is substantially cheaper to rent than to buy. But even in cities where you can have a mortgage payment for less than what you'd shell out for an apartment, it still may not make sense to own.

What many first-time buyers neglect to include in their budgets are the taxes, fees, insurance, and home repairs that come with owning a home. Many first-time buyers drain their accounts on the down payment and closing costs, leaving little for the actual year-to-year expenses of owning a home. This leaves many feeling "house poor" for the first few years.

Homeownership only works as a wealth-building strategy if you buy a house that you can comfortably afford, which means having enough cash in the bank to float the purchase as well as keeping an emergency fund to maintain the home after you close.

You Expect Your Family to Change Significantly

Ah, the idea of a starter home... Something small and reasonably priced that you can buy, decorate however you want, and sell when you're ready to move on. It seems like a win-win-win, but what if you meet someone a year after you buy and decide to move in together—only to find your perfect apartment is too small to happily accommodate you both? What if you're surprised by Baby #2? There are a million ways to blow the five-year homeownership timeline and end up losing money on your home, so think strategically instead of with emotion when making the decision to buy.

You'll Have Less Flexibility

If you are single and unattached, you have unlimited flexibility. You can easily take that big promotion in another state if you want to, or attempt to start your own business. This is your time in life to chase down whatever your heart desires, unencumbered. Would you jeopardize that by having a home to consider as well? Even though you can rent out a home and move if you absolutely had to, homeownership does mean that you're not as free to hop around as you'd like.

And what if you can't find a tenant? Most homeowners do not earn their money back before the five-year mark, which is why I encourage would-be buyers to consider where they see themselves in the near future before they commit to a mortgage.

You'll Have to Deal With Home Maintenance

This reason to put off buying a home has more to do with your personality than with your finances or five-to-ten year life plan. How do you want to spend your days? When you own a home you become your own landlord, repairman, contractor, and landscaper, all in one. Learning new skills can be fun, but home maintenance is also incredibly time consuming. If you love getting your hands dirty and being handy around the house, homeownership may be ideal for you.

If you love living a low maintenance lifestyle where you don't have to worry about home upkeep, mowing the lawn on a Saturday, or waiting for the plumber on your day off, keep your simple lifestyle and forgo homeownership for a spell.

You'll Have Less "Fun Money"

Aside from your lifestyle, your purchasing decisions will shift when you become a homeowner. Even if you buy a home that sits comfortably within your budget, you'll have to start paying for repairs, taxes, and any future home upgrades. You'll also typically shell out more to furnish your home than you did when you were a renter. These aren't drastic expenses, but I often miss the days when I could spend $300 on clothes instead of getting the brick exterior of my home pressure washed.

I won't bore you with specifics, but the bottom line is your bottom line will change. You won't have as much discretionary (read: play) money once you buy a home and it's important to account for this when making your decision.

You'll Make Slower Progress on Financial Goals

It can be tricky to balance student loan debt in post-grad life. In fact, a heavy student loan burden is often blamed for why many millennials are delaying homeownership in the first place. Even though buying a home is often considered a smart financial move, coming up with a hefty down payment and closing costs often means delaying other financial goals—like making significant contributions to savings or paying down student loan debt.

You'll Have Less Time for Travel & Other Adventures

It isn't just travel—having a mortgage may mean that you can't take that leap and start your own business. It may mean that your cash is tied up so you can't take that sabbatical in Italy, or attend conferences in your industry. Having a home will build your net worth, but it also means that a lot of your net worth isn't liquid and easily accessible for new opportunities.

Why You Need to Stay in Your Home For Five Years

Because of the way mortgages are structured, the first few years you are mainly paying off interest and not much principal. (*Principal* is the amount that you initially borrowed from the bank.) A portion of an amortization schedule for a $130,000 mortgage at 3.75% interest is provided on the following page.

Date	Payment	Principal	Interest	Total Int.	Balance
Sept. '16	$602.05	$195.80	$406.25	$406.25	$129,607.79
Oct. '16	$602.05	$196.41	$405.64	$811.89	$129,607.79
Nov. '16	$602.05	$197.03	$405.02	$1,216.91	$129,410.76
Dec. '16	$602.05	$197.64	$404.41	$1,621.32	$129,213.12
Jan. '17	$602.05	$198.26	$403.79	$2,025.11	$129,014.86
Feb. '17	$602.05	$198.88	$403.17	$2,428.28	$128,815.98
Mar. '17	$602.05	$199.50	$402.55	$2,830.83	$128,616.48
April '17	$602.05	$200.12	$401.93	$3,232.76	$128,416.36
May '17	$602.05	$200.75	$401.30	$3,634.06	$128,215.61
June '17	$602.05	$201.38	$400.67	$4,034.73	$128,014.23
July '17	$602.05	$202.01	$400.04	$4,434.78	$127,812.23
Aug. '17	$602.05	$202.64	$399.41	$4,834.19	$127,609.59
Sept. '17	$602.05	$203.27	$398.78	$5,232.97	$127,406.32
Oct. '17	$602.05	$203.91	$398.14	$5,631.12	$127,202.41
Nov. '17	$602.05	$204.54	$397.51	$6,028.62	$126,997.87
Dec. '17	$602.05	$205.18	$396.87	$6,425.49	$126,792.69
Jan. '18	$602.05	$205.82	$396.23	$6,821.72	$126,586.87
Feb. '18	$602.05	$206.47	$395.58	$7,217.30	$126,380.40
Mar. '18	$602.05	$207.11	$394.94	$7,612.24	$126,173.29
April '18	$602.05	$207.76	$394.29	$8,006.53	$125,965.53
May '18	$602.05	$208.41	$393.64	$8,400.18	$125,757.12
June '18	$602.05	$209.06	$392.99	$8,793.17	$125,548.06
July '18	$602.05	$209.71	$392.34	$9,185.51	$125,338.35
Aug. '18	$602.05	$210.37	$391.68	$9,577.19	$125,127.98
Sept. '18	$602.05	$211.03	$391.02	$9,968.21	$124,916.96

You will not be paying equal amounts of principal and interest until year five. Yikes! It's basically the same as renting until that time, and if you sold early, you might lose money once you account for closing and moving costs. This is why it's recommended that homebuyers stay in their homes for a few years. Homeownership is not the kind of thing that you can hop in and out of to make money.

How to Determine if You're Emotionally Ready

Have I scared you off yet? I hope not. I certainly didn't mean to. I just don't think that homeownership is something that should be entered into lightly, and yes, this opinion comes from my own experience of not taking the process seriously when I first bought. HGTV makes it look cool, but it's also a commitment. And if you're a young, hip, millennial-on-the-move, you may not need that kind of commitment in your life.

According to real estate company Redfin, one in four homeowners experience buyer's remorse. I don't want that for you, so here are a few signs that show you're actually ready to take the plunge.

You Love Your Location

...Like, "see yourself growing old there" kind of love.

You Have a Secure Job That You Like

I know we can't always foresee layoffs or changes in the workplace that will make us want to find a new job, but if you have a job that you're happy with and can see yourself at the company for a while, then you're definitely ready to commit to both your career and the area.

You're Willing to Give Up Certain Things to Buy a Home

If everything I've written hasn't scared you off, then yes, you might be ready to buy a home. Perhaps you love the idea of truly making something your own, or you're ready to start a family and put down roots. Either way, when you're ready and want to buy... you just know it in your bones.

You're Excited About This Next Step

You spend all of your time on Zillow or Redfin looking at homes in your area. You daydream about what your life will be like as a homeowner and you're so ready to leave behind all of the annoying things that come with being a renter, like lack of privacy, annoying HOA stipulations, and rent increases. You love the idea of being able to put your money toward something you'll own at the end of the day, rather than kissing that rent check goodbye each month.

However, if you're going through the process of buying a home—maybe you're already working with an agent or talking with a bank—and something feels "off," listen to that feeling. Your gut often knows things long before your head and heart do. Those feelings of hesitation are clear signs that now may not be the right time to buy. It's a huge commitment and one that you should enter into when you're feeling excited about the journey ahead.

But What About My Finances?

We'll cover preparing financially for homeownership in depth in Chapter Two, I promise. For now, here's a quick-and-dirty rundown of the basic qualifications you should have before you begin thinking about buying a home.

Good Credit

Your credit doesn't have to be perfect, but it should be decent. You can still get approved for a home with less-than-stellar credit, but your interest rate will be higher (and we're talking about interest on hundreds of thousands of dollars). It's in your best interest to have the highest credit score possible when applying for a mortgage because this is the number one way to save money on a new home. I'll cover a few tried-and-true ways to boost your credit score in Chapter Two.

A Healthy Nest Egg

Your "nest egg" is not just the savings you'll use to make your down payment. Instead, it's the money that you have set aside in a separate fund to cover legitimate emergencies that occur once you move into your home.

The Ability to Still Contribute to Other Financial Goals

Your income should be enough to accommodate your house payment and contribute to paying off debt, building savings (or let's be real, rebuilding them after the home purchase), and saving for retirement.

The Ability to Afford a Home in Your Desired Area

Not every area is affordable. Ironically, the metro areas with the strongest employment prospects are among the most expensive places to live, making it difficult for a millennial to recoup her money on a home purchase in the short term. My recommendation is to research the *Zillow Breakeven Horizon*, which is a quarterly index that measures how long you would have to live in a home before buying it would become more financially advantageous than renting it.

Location	Population Rank	Median Breakeven Horizon
New York, NY	1	2.9 years
Los Angeles, CA	2	3.5 years
Chicago, IL	3	2.0 years
Dallas, TX	4	1.2 years
Philadelphia, PA	5	2.5 years
Houston, TX	6	1.4 years
Washington, DC	7	3.6 years
Miami, FL	8	2.4 years

Source: Zillow.com data for Q1 2016.

This is why many millennials in urban areas have a hard time breaking into the real estate market. Between sky-high rent and increased living expenses like groceries, entertainment, and utilities, it can be hard to save for a down payment. Plus, even if you can afford homeownership (#ballerstatus), it may not be a great investment if you're planning to move before the breakeven horizon.

Few, if Any, Bad Financial Habits

No one is perfect with her finances all the time. (In fact, my blog, FinancialBestLife.com, formerly *L Bee and the Money Tree*, is built upon this very idea!) But if you want to make an adult purchase like a home, you'll need to exhibit more adult behavior with your money, too. You should be paying your bills on time (all of the time), and you should be done with over drafting your checking account and carrying balances on your credit cards. You should also be able to set and maintain a budget. I don't mean to bum you out, but these steps will be crucial to your financial success as a homeowner.

Steady Employment

From a financial perspective, you'll need to demonstrate to the bank that you're a loan-worthy person. After all, they're giving you a boatload of cash as a loan! It's a risk for them, so they want to make sure they're making the safest bet possible.

Don't even think about applying for a home loan if you don't have two years of steady, verifiable employment. You can still get a mortgage if you're self-employed, but more documentation will be required. I'll cover this more in depth in Chapter Two, as well.

....

Okay, so we've covered how to determine if you're ready to buy a home, and some of the indicators that you may (or may not) be primed for the homeownership journey ahead. If you're ready, then keep reading. It only gets more exciting from here!

CHAPTER 2

Financially Preparing for Homeownership

Before we begin going over the ins and outs of the homebuying process, we need to talk about what it takes to financially prepare for homeownership. For most, the act of financially preparing for homeownership should start a full year before earnestly beginning the search.

Here's how to prepare your finances for the biggest purchase of your lifetime.

Step 1: Pay Down Debt

With student loans and stagnant wages for millennials, it's no longer realistic to expect homebuyers to be debt-free before buying a home. But if you have a lot of debt, paying it down is one of the most important steps you can take to prepare your finances for homeownership. Otherwise, you'll drown.

Paying down debt has big homebuying benefits: It raises your credit score and frees up money in your budget for a mortgage payment and home upkeep. Everyone's relationship with debt and credit is different, but you'd be surprised how many people don't know the answers to these basic debt questions.

- Do you know the different types of debt that you're responsible for?
- Do you know your current debt balance?
- Do you know the interest rates?

Knowing answers to simple questions like these will help you understand how much you'll really pay in interest over the course of your debt repayment timeline.

Step 2: Fix Your Credit

Because of their young age, many millennials may have low (or no) credit, which means they'll have a hard time getting approved for a mortgage. For those who have no credit, try opening a credit card with a small limit and paying it off each month. For those with established credit, be sure to review your credit report, keep your balances below 30% of your credit limit, and pay all balances on time.

Here's the ultimate list of things to do to improve your credit before you start shopping for a home.

Keep Up With Your Credit Score and Credit Report

When it comes down to it, the best thing you can do to improve your credit score is to be aware of how your credit decisions impact it. Also, if you're planning to buy a home in the near future, order a hard copy of your credit report (you're entitled to one free copy every year) and look for errors and inaccuracies. If something is wrong it is eligible for removal!

Don't Close Old Credit Cards... Or Open New Ones

You've likely heard the phrase "use it or lose it," right? Well, that is the exact opposite of what you should be doing to maintain a healthy credit score. Since credit scores include factors such as average age of accounts and debt-to-income ratios, keeping older credit lines open—including cards that you have paid off—will help your overall credit utilization. Pay off your cards, but keep them open so that your average "age of credit" is higher. Once you close a card, the age on that account goes away!

It looks much better to potential lenders to see that you have kept a card a longer time and with a lower balance than to only see the shiny new store credit card you recently opened to snag a deal. You also shouldn't open new cards when looking to buy a home because—you guessed it—this drags down the age of your credit history as well.

Applying for new credit products also means that lenders will do a "hard pull" of your credit. Having too many of these inquiries in a six-to-twelve month timeframe can be a major red flag to mortgage lenders, as it indicates you need money and have a hard time paying down debts.

Avoid High Credit Utilization

Paying off debt is the best way to reduce your credit utilization. Having multiple credit products can look good on your report, but not if they're all maxed out. Your credit utilization rate should be below 30% of your total credit limit for each card—meaning it may be a good idea to whittle down the balances of cards over that rate first before completely paying them all off.

Another way to decrease your utilization—without having to pay off a large portion of debt—is to contact your lender to see about a credit limit increase.

Don't Co-Sign for Loans

You might feel like you're helping your family member/friend/college roommate by co-signing for a loan, but it can end up being a financial misstep for both of you. When co-signing a loan, you're essentially saying that if the other co-signer isn't able to make the payments, then you will take responsibility and pay. That's a big commitment, and if you're considering buying a home, now is the time to focus on your own credit.

Avoid Making Late Payments

Don't ever get comfortable paying late on a credit product. Even if you're not being charged a late fee, your on-time payment percentage will suffer the longer you wait. You want your credit to be pristine when applying for a mortgage!

A helpful way to stop forgetting about making payments is to set up reminders or automate your minimum payment for the same time each month. You can always make additional payments if you want to put more toward a particular debt, but automating the minimum will keep you from the late payment repercussions.

Step 3: Save Up for the Down Payment

What about that down payment? If you don't have a large nest egg or a gift from family members, it's time to start trimming the budget and saving aggressively.

Get Budget Friendly

Saying that you're going to put a certain amount of money toward debt each month is great, but it may be harder to achieve if you're chronically strapped for cash. I recommend updating your budget any time you have a big financial priority change like debt repayment or buying a home. By tracking your money this way, you'll notice all the weird stuff you spend too much money on each month!

No one likes to be the party pooper who can't afford to go out for drinks, but it's sometimes a necessary evil when you're trying to cut back. Learning to say no to temptation (and friends) can be hard, but it will help to keep your eye on the prize: Being able to make a nice down payment on your first home.

I recommend doing a quarterly or biannual audit of your utility bills and other fixed expenses to identify potential areas of savings. Start by taking one morning each month to call your utility companies and talk to them about lowering your bills. Here's where I was able to nab additional savings the last time I did my own utility audit.

- Mortgage: Decreased from $904 to $853 per month, saving $51. Once I had finally become 20% vested in my home, I asked my lender to take the private mortgage insurance (PMI) premium off my monthly tab. Private mortgage insurance is required by lenders when home-buyers put less than 20% down. So if you're planning to do this, expect to see this extra fee on your monthly mortgage payment.

- Cable: Decreased from $117 to $84 per month, saving $33. I did this by finally cutting cable and keeping just my internet bill.
- Security System: Decreased from $48 to $38 per month, saving $10.
- Car Insurance: Decreased from $163 to $116 per month, saving $47. I previously had both my home and car insurance with one company, thinking they were giving me the best deal. After lots of homework, I found out that I *did* have the best price on homeowners insurance, but I could get a much lower rate on car insurance by switching to another provider.

Making these small tweaks allowed me to put $141 back into my budget each month. Imagine what would happen if you put that money into your down payment savings account?

Just an FYI: A utility audit is a large time investment. You have to create a plan of attack, otherwise you'll go crazy in a circle of hell where you're listening to automated customer service systems on loop. The time and effort involved is the number one reason why most of us don't get around to a yearly audit of our fixed expenses.

Look Into Down Payment Assistance

The smartest financial move that I made when purchasing my first home was in thoroughly researching every down payment assistance and grant program that I could find. In 2013, the city of Atlanta was offering $15,000 in down payment assistance grants to first-time homebuyers who purchased foreclosures in certain neighborhoods. So I received a "soft loan" for $15,000, meaning a portion of the amount is forgiven each year. I could use the money however I chose—for the down payment, closing costs, or principal. This is why I only had to pay $1,800 at closing, plus $500 in earnest money.

Your mortgage broker or real estate agent may mention down payment assistance programs to you, but it always makes sense to search for programs that you may qualify for. To get started, Google the phrase "[state you live in] down payment assistance programs." Boom! Knowledge!

Be sure to exhaust every avenue. Are you a veteran? Single mother? You may qualify for additional grants and funds from your city or state. Now isn't the time to be shy. Make it a priority to talk to local lenders to learn more about the assistance options in your area.

For any assistance program that you're considering, it's important to read the fine print to understand how much assistance you'll be receiving, as well as the expectations and repayment requirements (if any). Ideally, you'd want your program to allow for funds to be used at closing, as this is where most first-time buyers incur unexpected expenses.

....

A note about down payment assistance: Some programs (like mine) require you to buy a home in a certain zip code in order to qualify for the moolah. In the case of the assistance that I received, I was only eligible if I bought in a neighborhood hit hard by foreclosures. This is a dainty way of saying, "up and coming," which is a daintier way of saying, "run down." Folks definitely comment on my neighborhood when they visit, but I've never had a problem and the neighborhood has turned around a lot in just a few years' time.

....

The Bank of Mom and Dad

Don't qualify for assistance programs or have any available in your area? You can always consider hitting up Mom and Dad for a gift. (As of the time this book went to press, in 2016 your parents could gift up to $14,000 per person—or $28,000 for you and your spouse—and still stay within the annual gift-tax exclusion.) Because it's a "gift," they can't tell you how to use it, but I know a few millennials who have used cash from "the Bank of Mom and Dad" to help cover the down payment or closing costs on their first homes.

Because of stricter financing terms following the 2008 housing crash, I recommend leveraging the money for closing and moving costs rather than factoring it into your down payment. Why? This helps ensure that you only buy a home you can reasonably afford. Also, for lenders, having a down payment at the ready suggests you're less likely to default on your loan, whereas using a gift to make your down payment can be a red flag and make it more difficult to get pre-approved.

From my own experience, I've seen a friend make an offer on a home, have the offer accepted, and then have to back out and lose the earnest money because the bank had concerns about the large gift from Mom and Dad.

But don't let the difficulty discourage you. If you have a gift from Mom and Dad that you'd like to use for your down payment, you'll simply need to document the process (i.e., the actual financial transaction between you and your parents) very, very well. You'll be required to provide the following paperwork to be pre-approved for the loan:

- Gift letter: A standard form that states who gave you the money, when, and why, plus the amount that you received.
- Proof of transfer: A copy of the check, wire transfer, or money order that shows how the money was delivered into your account. These are very easy to acquire!
- Bank statement: The bank needs proof that your parents have the funds they are gifting to you. The statement should include their names, account number, and balance.
- Deposit receipt: You'll need to provide a receipt for the deposit of the funds and make sure that the account number of your parents' bank matches the bank statement they submitted.

Step 4: Get Pre-Qualified for a Mortgage

You should get pre-qualified for a mortgage before you begin seriously shopping (read: touring homes instead of just browsing online) so that you know how much home you can actually afford. As a bonus, being pre-qualified also lets sellers and agents know that you mean business—and best of all, it's 100% free to rate shop!

What Kind of Loan Should I Get Pre-Qualified For?

You don't have to put 20% down in order to purchase a home; there are banks that will offer you loans for much less down as long as you have good credit. However, if your credit is less than stellar and you'd like to purchase a home with less of a down payment, you should look into an FHA loan, which is insured by the Federal Housing Administration and has less stringent credit requirements.

An FHA loan often entices buyers with sexy interest rates and lower down payments. (You can get an FHA loan with as little as 3.5% down!) It's a good option to consider if you're a first-timer with limited means to make a down payment.

With that said, there are a few downsides to purchasing a home with less than 20% down:

- You'll need to pay private mortgage insurance, which protects the lender if you default on your loan. The insurance usually costs between 0.15% to 2.50% of the loan amount and will be tacked onto your monthly payment.
- You may pay a higher interest rate, which can really add up over time.
- If you live in a hot real estate market where the inventory is low, putting less than 20% down may make your offer less attractive to sellers. If a homeowner receives multiple offers, they most often choose the one with the highest down payment or highest earnest money offering— or all-cash offers, which are even better—because those offers are viewed as having a lower risk of falling through due to financing issues.

How Do I Comparison Shop for Mortgages?

Most millennials will start shopping for a mortgage with their primary bank, where their checking and savings accounts are held. There's nothing wrong with this strategy, but it's important to obtain quotes from at least three different lenders to ensure that you're getting the lowest interest rate possible.

Your primary bank may not have the lowest rate, and even a small difference in rates could save you thousands of dollars over the life of the loan (typically, 30 years).

Yes, shopping for interest rates will put a few hard inquiries on your credit report, but these aren't a cause for concern. Why? Because credit bureaus expect that you'll want to rate shop and often treat multiple inquiries from home, auto, and student loan lenders as one inquiry. Isn't that nice? At most, a hard pull on your credit from a mortgage company will lower your score two to four points.

How Does the Pre-Approval Process Work?

The mortgage amount that you're pre-approved for largely depends on your debt-to-income (DTI) ratio. This number represents how much money you spend each month paying for your debts. There are two types of DTI numbers that banks look at: a front-end ratio and a back-end ratio.

The front-end ratio represents how much of your income goes toward paying for housing costs. If you rent, this is the amount that you pay in rent each month divided by your gross monthly income.

For example, if your monthly gross income is $3,500 and you spend $1,000 on rent, then your DTI front-end ratio is 29%.

The back-end ratio represents how much of your income goes toward all of your recurring debt payments.

For example, if your monthly gross income is $3,500 and you spend $300 on student loans, $250 on your auto loan, and $1,000 on rent, then your DTI back-end ratio is 44%.

To qualify for a conventional mortgage, you typically want your front-end ratio to be 28% or lower, and your back-end ratio to be 36% or lower.

....

The bottom line: You can't seriously shop for homes without knowing how much you can afford. Fortunately, getting pre-approved for a mortgage is surprisingly simple, with many lenders offering answers online within minutes. Use a free resource like Redfin's Home Affordability Calculator to play with the numbers and see how your monthly payment will vary, depending on your interest rate and the amount of money that you put down.

....

Step 5: Get Organized for the Mortgage Application

Real estate is a paperwork game. If you're not so great with keeping track of important documents, then I recommend pulling together the most important papers you'll need for the mortgage underwriting process in advance. There's no sense frantically searching for a paper and delaying your closing date if you don't have to.

Here's a small sample of what you'll need to pull: tax records, employment forms, W-2s, W-9s, and potentially even weirder demands like letters from former landlords, lovers (yes, this happened), and family members.

What If I'm Self-Employed?

Qualifying for a loan when you're self-employed is simply more difficult than when you have a traditional nine-to-five job. I know, it's totally unfair. You're stimulating the economy with your small business and here is BIG FINANCE heckling you for proof that you work hard for your money.

It's not insurmountable, but you'll need to gather more information than your corporate counterparts. Lenders will need you to prove that you have enough income to make your loan payments. The documents that you'll need to include are:

- A copy of your business license and articles of incorporation
- Profit and loss statements from the last two years
- Checking, savings, and retirement account statements
- Signed, dated individual tax returns, with all applicable tax schedules for the most recent two years
- For a C corporation, S corporation, or partnership: Signed, dated business tax returns, with all applicable tax schedules for the most recent two years
- For a C corporation or S corporation: Business credit report

A Few Final Tips on Preparing for Homeownership

Avoid big purchases. This is especially true for small business owners. Try to limit big business expenditures, and if you need to make a purchase or two, make sure it's from your business account and not your personal one.

Pro Tip: "Don't buy anything new from contract to close, as it could affect your credit," recommends David Davidson, a buyer's agent in Greenville, South Carolina. "I've seen washing machine purchases cost people a home because they bought and destroyed their original pre-approval information."

Save as much as you can. Even if you're just beginning to look for a home, it's important to save as much as you can because, without question, an unexpected expense or two will arise during the homebuying process. You'll also have to pay for an inspection and an appraisal, plus fees.

Stay at your current job. Unless it's the opportunity of a lifetime, it's typically frowned upon to make big life changes during the homebuying process, as this could affect how much you may be approved for when buying your first home. Similarly, if you're a parent and would like to stay at home while your spouse works, wait until after the purchase to evaluate this big financial move.

Pay all your bills on time. If you're responsible enough to consider homeownership, you probably have no problem paying your bills on time. Still, shopping for a home can be stressful, so it's important to keep track of all your bills during a time when your personal finances are about to be scrutinized by the bank. Now is not the time to pay a bill late.

Now let's move on to the good stuff—everything you want in that gorgeous first home of yours!

CHAPTER 3

---•---

Getting Started With Your Home Search

I don't like to play favorites with my writing, but this chapter is definitely the most fun I've written. Why? Because this is where you get to brainstorm all of the amazing things that you want in your dream home. And then I'm going to tell you how to get started making those dreams a reality. What can be more fun than a chapter dedicated to that?

Nothing. Except maybe a puppy party.

In the previous chapter you learned how to get your finances organized for your home purchase. Now it's time to put that knowledge on the back burner for a bit and figure out what it is that you truly want to buy. Here are the seven steps to getting started with your home search.

Step 1: Narrow Down Your Ideal Location

I moved to New York at the age of twenty-three, and after living in the city for two years, I decided to move back home to Atlanta. Having had the experience of living far away from home was amazing because it taught me what I did and did not want from my life, my career, and my living situation.

I knew that moving back South was for the long haul, so I felt comfortable with the decision to put down some official—and expensive—roots. Even though buying such a large home without thinking about shifting circumstances is something that I wish I'd done differently, I don't regret my initial move to look for something permanent.

Before you start looking for a home, spend some time thinking about what you want your life to look like and where your ideal home is located. It will make all the difference when it comes to feeling confident about your purchase. After you home in on where you want to lay down roots, it's time to roll up your sleeves and figure out how much you can afford.

Step 2: Determine Your Price Range

As I mentioned in Chapter Two, it is strongly recommended that you get pre-qualified for a mortgage before you link up with an agent and start touring homes. (In fact, most decent agents will not work with you unless you have a pre-approval letter!) When you're beginning your home search, you're likely to go online and browse first, but how can you know how much home you can truly afford?

Typically a homebuyer will be approved for a mortgage that is about three times her annual salary, but there are a variety of other factors involved in determining how much home you can afford, such as the amount of money that you have for a down payment, the total amount of your monthly debt payments, and any other financial obligations like alimony or child support that you are responsible for.

There are also a wide variety of home affordability calculators available on the internet where you can plug in your data and receive a rough estimate of how much home you can afford. (Personally, I like Redfin's Home Affordability Calculator the best.)

Step 3: Build Your Wish List

Okay! Yes! Now we're getting to the best part.

Everyone has a wish list for what they want in a home, whether they're currently looking, in a home already, or still renting and compiling a list of "must haves" for the future.

....

Before I purchased, I'd been making a list in my head of everything that I wanted in a home since I was ten years old. I still think about the features my one day "forever home" will have. It's fun for those lazy afternoons on Pinterest.

....

If you watch plenty of *House Hunters* episodes on HGTV, then you'll know that wish lists don't always line up with budgets, but it's still good to have a rough idea of what you'd like before you aggressively begin to search. A wish list will also help your agent find homes best suited to your needs.

You can start with a very basic wish list, but ask yourself: What are the absolute deal breakers? And if you're shopping with your spouse or partner, discuss what each of you is willing to sacrifice for the team.

Step 4: Start Online

Once you have your wish list in hand, go crazy looking at homes online. Seriously, I mean it. Knock yourself out. Depending upon your price range, location goals, and flexibility, you may find yourself looking through hundreds of listings in your area.

When I was shopping I wrote down ten homes at a time that I wanted to consider and then did all of the steps outlined in Step 5. This helped me narrow my total list of homes that I was seriously considering from about thirty to between five and seven. You'll be surprised by how many homes you'll be able to cross off your list just by doing a little recon on your own.

Step 5: Narrow Down Your List Before Touring

It wasn't just the down payment assistance I received that led me to the particular home I bought in 2013. Having worked for a hedge fund, I knew how to do thorough research, otherwise known as due diligence, on a potential investment. (In this case, my first home!)

Before I scheduled a showing with my real estate agent, I took a day to drive by my list of potential properties that had looked good online. I drove by during the day, at night, and in both the morning and afternoon rush hour to gauge traffic.

Because I was using down payment assistance and specifically looking at distressed properties, I was able to vet homes just by looking at their exteriors. Many of them were in bad shape. While this may not be the case for the homes that you're interested in, I still recommend a pre-tour drive-by.

You may notice a few issues with a particular home during your drive-by that weren't noted or pictured on the internet listing. Perhaps the home is located next to something that doesn't work for you, like a noisy business or construction zone.

Best of all, this homework can be done on your own time, so you're only truly visiting homes with your agent that you have vetted; making the most of your time together.

Speaking of real estate agents, have you found one yet?

Step 6: Find an Agent

Real estate agents are salespeople by nature—they know how to make a good first impression—but it's important to get to know your agent and interview her before agreeing to work together. Why? Because the most expensive purchase of your lifetime is in your agent's hands, and it's important that you feel comfortable with her for two reasons:

1. As a first-time buyer you'll have lots of questions. You want someone who respects the fact that as a first-timer you'll need a bit of education. Feeling comfortable enough to ask your agent questions (even if they're a little basic) is important.
2. You need to trust that she will have your best interests at heart when negotiating with the seller's agent on your behalf. Having an organized and prompt agent can

mean the difference between your dream home and "the one that got away."

I found my agent on the internet and I did not meet with her before we began touring homes. She was fast and responsive during the contract and bidding process, but we didn't interact much and I definitely didn't feel comfortable asking her questions. The experience would have been better if I had taken the time to interview a handful of agents and asked them (either via phone or email) a series of interview questions to get to know them better and understand how we'd work together.

To help you along in your own search, here is a list of questions that you should ask an agent during an initial interview.

How many sales have you handled in my area?

You'll want to find a real estate agent who knows the market conditions in your area because she will know the best locations, comparable prices, and what to expect during the bidding process.

What is your fee?

Some agents charge less, but the home seller typically pays 6% of the final sale price to both of the real estate agents involved: 3% goes to the seller's agent and 3% goes to the buyer's agent. As a buyer, you should never pay your agent up front and should be leery of any agent who suggests such an arrangement.

When am I committed to working with you?

This question may seem a little confusing, so let's break it down. Many homebuyers start touring homes, perhaps with the listing agent or someone "on call" the day they submitted the contact form online, without realizing this can obligate them to working with that agent. You want to hire your own agent, and not someone that you just happened to meet because you toured a home.

When working with an agent, he or she will require you to sign a buyer's agency agreement. Typically, this agreement lasts from three to twelve months, but you can negotiate the length of time that feels comfortable to you.

What if I'm unhappy with your service?

There's actually a lot of ways that working with a real estate agent can go wrong, mostly because at the end of the day, an agent only gets paid when you *buy.* This can lead to pushy sales tactics, underhanded negotiations with sellers and other agents, and a lack of communication because your agent is out chasing other sales. It happens.

So, with that in mind, be sure to ask your agent if she's willing to guarantee your satisfaction (this is a tip from my friends at Redfin!) and what you will be allowed to do in the event you want to "fire" your agent.

Step 7: Keep an Open Mind When Touring Homes

If you're a millennial with a limited budget—which, let's face it, most of us are—your first home probably won't be your dream home with everything just the way you like it. Things like paint colors, fixtures, and finishes can easily be changed, so go in with an open mind about the possibilities and potential, and not just what you see in front of you. Once you find the home that you want, be sure to do the following:

Bid Appropriately and Unemotionally

Ask your agent to research comparable properties in your area before you make a bid. Once you know the average selling price for similar homes, consider making an offer a little bit lower in case the seller wants to negotiate.

Try to avoid a bidding war at all costs. In my own experience, a bidding war becomes more about emotion than good common sense. Sometimes it's unavoidable if you're shopping in an area where inventory is low, but before making an offer decide the maximum amount that you're willing to pay if this situation arises.

Also remember that when there is competition, the highest offer isn't always the one that wins. Sellers are looking for a quick, simple close, so if you have an all-cash offer, a significant down payment, or can close faster than other potential buyers, you'll likely win.

If you're interested in a certain home, your agent may recommend writing a letter introducing your family. Because homebuying is so emotional, many sellers love to hear that their beloved home is going to someone who also wants to love the house. You never know!

Sleep On It

I never make big financial decisions without a good night's sleep, and you shouldn't either. In the event of competition, many real estate agents will suggest that you make an offer right away—often immediately after touring the home. I find this very overwhelming and recommend giving yourself at least one night to think about what you really want and, most importantly, how much you're willing to pay in the event that you do want to make an offer.

Don't Skimp on the Extra Homework

Never stop learning about your new home. Before I bought my home, I read press releases and news articles about activity in the area, and I spent time in the neighborhood and the parks. I also went to the neighborhood association meeting—if you're looking to buy in an "up and coming neighborhood," make sure that it has an active neighborhood association! Do all of your homework so that you're not unpleasantly surprised by anything once you move in.

Avoid Purchasing More Home Than You Can Afford

This is the key to being a successful millennial homeowner. While you have a lower salary, large student loan payments, and limited savings, it's important that you buy a home you can comfortably afford.

Think of how your mortgage, property taxes, fees, insurance, and home maintenance costs will fit in your budget as a homeowner. Homeownership is smart, but it can also be expensive if you don't prepare.

And remember, just because your lender approved you for a certain amount doesn't mean that you have to buy up to that limit.

House hunting is exciting. Truly. But it is also exhausting.

....

Here's my final and favorite tip: The more homework that you do on the front end, the less frustrated you'll be during the home shopping process itself. By doing logical, methodical detective work on your potential home, you'll be able to make smarter decisions and avoid any messy, emotional complications.

....

CHAPTER 4

—•—

When You Are Under Contract

So you've found the home of your dreams, put in an offer, negotiated with the seller, and now you're "under contract." Congrats!

You may think the hard work is over, but being under contract—the time period before you've "closed" on your loan at the bank—is often the trickiest part of the process for first-time buyers.

Why?

Because you don't know what's happening. The bank is scrutinizing your financials so they can approve you for the funds you're asking for, but there's a lot of technical terms and jargon associated with this process that you may not fully understand.

You'll also sign numerous documents at closing and may not completely comprehend all of it. That's okay. This chapter is here to help!

What to Expect When You're Under Contract

You've found the house that you want and now you're under contract, but the home isn't totally yours...yet. Depending on the amount of time that your real estate agent was able to negotiate for you, the pending sale will immediately go into a due diligence period once the seller accepts your offer.

This period (typically between ten and fourteen business days) includes an inspection, an appraisal, and doing additional research so that you feel confident in your purchase. The section below details what will happen step-by-step once the seller accepts your offer.

You'll Put Down Earnest Money

During the real estate transaction, you will need to pay the seller earnest money, which is essentially a deposit that reaffirms your interest in purchasing the home. After all, the seller is taking her home off the market because you said you wanted it! In the event that you end up backing out of the purchase after the due diligence period is over, the seller will get to keep your earnest money for the hardship. But if you decide not to buy within the due diligence window, you get to keep the money.

Typically the earnest money amount is between 1% to 2% of the total purchase price of the home. You don't turn it over to the seller directly, however; earnest money is always held in a separate account (usually with the closing attorney) to avoid disputes.

You'll Get (And Should Attend!) an Inspection

Since you'll be paying an inspector to do a walk-through of your home and prepare a written report of the findings, I've known many homeowner friends who have decided to skip the inspection and just read the report. No! Bad! Wrong!

The inspection is for *you*. In addition to finding out if anything is wrong with the home, this is your chance to learn where the breaker box and water main are located, where the shut-off valves are, etc. Plus, being present guarantees a more thorough inspection. (People behave differently when they're being watched—it is proven.) To begin the inspection process you should:

- Find a qualified inspector through friends or Angie's List, and ask to see a sample final report before hiring. The report should be thorough, with at least fifteen pages of documentation and photos.
- Once the inspection process is complete, get estimates for the items noted in the report that need to be fixed. Then you can ask the seller to make the necessary changes or provide a credit at closing to cover the costs.

If any game-changing news comes to light during an inspection, then you're able to walk away if you think the home isn't worth the trouble. This is why it's important to get a home inspection ASAP!

You'll Get an Appraisal

Since the housing crash of 2008, many lenders have tightened their terms and will no longer approve a mortgage on a home that doesn't appraise for at least that value, regardless of how much you're willing to pay for it. This can frustrate a buyer who falls in love with a home, but does not have enough cash to cover the difference between the seller's asking price and the appraisal. An appraisal can also be devastating to a seller who puts a lot of work into her home, but isn't seeing the value reflected in the appraisal.

....

If you don't have enough cash to cover the difference between the asking price and the appraisal, and you can't come to an agreement with the seller on a lower asking price, then you'll want to be able to walk away from the transaction and still get your earnest money back.

....

You'll Have to Get Your Documents Together

If all goes well with the inspection and the appraisal, then you're one step closer to closing on your dream home. Once the due diligence window has passed, the bank will verify your financials and begin preparing the funds for disbursement.

Here are a few of the standard documents that you will be asked to provide during the loan underwriting process:

- Check stubs for the past three months
- Tax returns and W-2s for the last two years
- Any additional proof of income that you may have, such as your stock portfolio, alimony, child support, etc.
- Bank statements for the past three months
- A letter stating your employment and rental history for the past two years
- A homebuyer seminar certificate of completion
- Any documentation from your parents if you received a large financial gift
- Copies of all rent checks paid to your current landlord

If you have a side hustle or work for yourself you'll also need to provide:

- Copies of all checks that you have received from clients
- PayPal statements from the last three months

If you're planning to buy a home and don't know where these documents are located, then I suggest trying to find them immediately! I was able to access my files quickly and turn them over to my mortgage broker within a matter of hours—if not minutes—whenever he asked for them by following these key pieces of advice:

- Get digital. Now, I know it will be difficult for some of you to let go of paper (I'm a keep-a-hard-copy-for-my-records kinda gal, too), but when your mortgage company is asking for these documents, it's easier to point, click, and email a PDF than to scan all of your documents at once.
- If you're thinking about purchasing a home in the next six to twelve months, thin out your files. I cut down on my files just by scanning and digitizing my pay stubs for the past two years.
- Create a master list of all your accounts and passwords.
- Once you've been pre-approved and are under contract on a house, keep a copy of everything the bank sends you via email or snail mail.

You'll Have to Pad Your Budget

You're preparing to close on your home and shell out thousands of dollars for the down payment and the closing costs, so you know that now isn't the time to get all loosey-goosey with your budget. You should pay special attention to your budget during the "under contract" phase of a home purchase because there are many, many fees that may surprise you. Here's a list of the fees that I incurred and the dollar amounts that you can expect to pay:

- Earnest money: $500 to $1,000
- Home inspection: $300 to $500
- Home appraisal: $400 to $500
- Document preparation fees: $250 paid to an attorney at closing
- Cashier's check fee and postage: $30
- Homebuyer education class: $15
- HUD consultant fee: $4,000 to $5,000 paid at the outset of the renovation if you're buying a foreclosure and using a 203(k) renovation loan

That's a few thousand dollars out of pocket just to get to closing. Yikes! The moral of the story is to pay attention to your budget so that you won't have to put these fees on a credit card.

You'll Pay Closing Costs

What exactly should you expect to pay at closing? Well, buyers and sellers typically pay different things on closing day. Sellers will cover the commission for real estate agents and title transfer fees, while buyers have all sorts of itemized costs related to the mortgage. Here's a quick-and-dirty list of what you, as a buyer, will be expected to cover at closing.

- Administrative fees: These fees can be as basic as a processing fee, notary fee, or a fee for obtaining your credit report.
- Loan fees: Yes, there are even fees on the mortgage loan itself! Much like a student loan or other large personal loan, your mortgage has fees that will be lumped into your closing costs. Along with signing a promissory note (your legal IOU), you'll also likely pay an origination fee for your mortgage loan. This is a charge for the processing of your loan and is typically between 1% to 5% of your total loan amount.
- Insurances and taxes: If you're buying a home close to the end of the property tax season, you'll need to prepare to pay that charge upfront. Also keep in mind any homeowner association fees that need to be paid.
- The down payment: Although most experts suggest that you put down 20% of the home's purchase price, there are new types of mortgage products and down payment assistance programs that allow you to pay less out of pocket when purchasing your first home. Refer to Chapter Two for more details.

Keep in mind that all of these expenses should be set in stone in advance of your actual closing date. If you have any questions or concerns be sure to discuss with your lender.

It may also be worth discussing closing costs with the seller. If it's a buyer's market—too many homes for sale, not enough buyers—then you could possibly negotiate for the seller to pay some or all of your closing costs.

So, What Actually Happens During Closing?

You've found the perfect home, submitted all the paperwork, and have been approved for a loan. Now what? With all the chaos that can surround purchasing a home, it can be hard to see the light at the end of the tunnel. Especially when that light comes with terms and conditions.

But soon the day you've been waiting for will come: closing day. This is when you'll pay the required fees, sign the paperwork, and (typically) get the keys to your new home. Unfortunately, it's a little more complicated than just showing up. I know you're excited, but stay focused for just a little while longer. Knowing what to expect on closing day will help you be aware of what you're signing, stamping, and ultimately paying for.

I'm about to throw a lot of information at you and I understand this all sounds very confusing and complicated. Bear with me! We are almost done. Here's what you can expect to sign on the day that you close on your home. (Note: Each city/state may have different requirements for what documents are needed at closing. Check with your agent for details.)

Pre-Closing Documents

At least three days before closing you'll receive closing disclosure and loan estimate documents. These will make the specifics of your loan and closing costs incredibly easy to understand. Think of these as mortgage fact sheets. They will include information like:

• The full loan amount, less your down payment
• The interest rate of your loan

- Your estimated total monthly payment broken down by principal, interest, PMI, and escrow amount (if you have an escrow account at your bank)
- Whether your loan includes a pre-payment penalty and/or any balloon payments
- An estimate of taxes, insurance, and property assessments that you'll pay (Even if you have an escrow account at the bank to handle these transactions, it's good to know this information, so don't skip it!)
- And my personal favorite: The total closing costs and cash that you'll need to close on your home. This is very important for you to take note of, as this is the amount that you'll need to bring with you to closing!

The bank sends you the closing disclosure and loan estimate in advance because they want you to spend time reviewing these documents before you close. Note if anything is different than what you expected, or if you're confused by a fee. Now is not the time to skip out on the homework—you're about to finalize this very big purchase! You can see examples of these forms at ConsumerFinance.gov to get an idea of what they look like.

Financial Documents to Sign at Closing

Buying a home is first and foremost a financial transaction. Here are some of the financial forms that you'll see at closing:

- Loan application: You completed a loan application when you first applied for your loan, remember? The bank will print out this application and verify that all of the financial information that you provided initially, like your salary and how much debt you have, is still correct. Then they'll ask you to review and sign at closing. If you now have a higher paying job or took out additional lines of credit between the time you applied for the loan and closing day, you'll have to inform the lender before signing this form.

- Mortgage: The mortgage is the amount of money you're borrowing from the bank to pay for your property. At closing you'll need to sign a document that says you are borrowing this money from the bank and that you're putting up the property itself as collateral. (This is why banks foreclose on properties when homeowners stop making mortgage payments.)
- Separate bill of sale: This is for any items that you're buying along with your home, including furniture, window treatments, appliances, etc.
- Promissory note: This document details the amount of your loan, the interest rate, the terms of any interest rate changes, and the terms of the loan itself.
- Deed of trust: This gives ownership to the new property owner. It is only used in homebuying transactions where a buyer is purchasing a home outright and not using a bank loan to fund the purchase. When you pay off your mortgage in fifteen or thirty years (or less if you're a financial ninja) the bank will mail you the deed. Once you have the deed, you can then transfer ownership of your home to your spouse or heirs in the event of your death.
- Transfer tax declarations: If you are going to be transferring property taxes and payments before the end of the tax year, both the buyer and seller must sign declarations disclosing the purchase price and related taxes at closing.

A Few Other Tips to Keep in Mind at Closing

It May Be Crowded

Depending on your state and the type of property you're buying, there may be quite a few people in the room when you sign your closing paperwork. In addition to yourself and the seller, prepare to see some combination of real estate agents and attorneys for both parties, a representative from your lender's company, a notary public, and a closing agent.

It may seem like too many cooks in the kitchen, but keep in mind that each person is a professional and needed to ensure a smooth transaction. They are at the closing to dot every "i" and cross every "t," and to make sure that both you and the seller understand every document that is being signed.

Come Prepared to Exchange Money

Remember when I told you to review your closing disclosure and loan estimate in advance to see how much cash you'll need at closing? You'll need to either prepare a cashier's check or wire transfer to make sure this money gets paid to the bank. Upon closing, your lender will also disburse the amount of your home loan to your closing agent to distribute to the seller.

Do a Final Review of the Paperwork

The biggest part of closing day will be signing all of the paperwork required for the home sale. But what exactly are you signing? Even though you were good and reviewed the documents before closing, spend time review-ing them one last time before you sign at the closing itself.

Make sure that all rates, amounts, and terms for your loan match what you previously agreed upon. Make sure that you are satisfied with your loan and, if not, don't sign until you are able to come to an agreement with your lender.

After all is said and done, you'll finally get your keys and can start moving in!

CHAPTER 5

The Many Surprises of Homeownership

This chapter includes the many things that you'll be surprised to learn during your first year of homeownership. But really, it's a chapter dedicated to all of the information that I wish I had known before buying my first home. I'm talking about those crazy, "I never would've thought of that!" details; the things that can completely throw you for a loop when entering into something as new, exciting, and darn expensive as homeownership. You're welcome.

I mentioned in the previous chapter that once your home is under contract you'll need to do an inspection. This is an absolute must even if you're buying a foreclosed home or other type of "as is" property. This is your time to get to know your future home—the ins and outs, what's great about it, and what you'll eventually need to fix.

I'm starting off the "surprises" chapter with more information about the inspection because, invariably, every home inspection is full of a surprise or two. Some of these surprises could derail your entire sale, which is why it's important to schedule the inspection ASAP (during your due diligence period), and for you to physically attend the inspection so you can learn firsthand what issues need to be addressed.

What to Look for During a Home Inspection

While looking at a property online might seem extensive enough, you don't want to buy only to discover you'll have to sink thousands of dollars into repairs. Home inspectors check for potential issues and repairs for both the seller and buyer so that the two sides can make further decisions about the home purchase, such as whether to lower the price or complete repairs before closing.

As I mentioned earlier, I bought a foreclosed home. What I saw during the walkthrough was literally what I got. Honestly, at the time I wasn't entirely sure what this meant—and the fact that I was buying it "as is" made me not look at the home as closely as I should have. Being a first-time homebuyer, I wasn't even aware of the things I should have been looking for during the inspection.

For example, I was so focused on the renovations that I was planning to do that I completely missed the fact that the home didn't have any plumbing. (Literally, the copper from the plumbing had been stolen while the house sat vacant.) This was a $9,000 fix, and looking back, that money definitely could have been spent elsewhere.

Everything during an inspection needs to be noted by you or the inspector, even if it doesn't seem like an emergency. Why? Because it represents money that you'll eventually have to spend somewhere down the line.

For example, take the condition of the stairs up to my attic. They were fine and didn't need to be immediately replaced, but the stair treads were loose and let a lot of cold air into the main floor of my house during the winter. I eventually replaced them, but if all of the things I needed to fix had really sunk in during the inspection, I doubt I would have purchased the home.

I also assumed that it was my inspector's job to educate me on what I should be looking at. This was totally wrong. I was walking around with him, and sure, he pointed out the big stuff, but I didn't ask enough questions or suggest that he investigate every corner for potential problems. Sometimes we have to demand an education.

Here are a handful of the most important issues to look for during an inspection. If you find any of these, you could be in for large estimates and costly repairs.

Water Damage

Water damage scares homeowners, and for good reason. This is because it means there is likely a leak somewhere in the home. By the time you open up walls and floors to find the leak, it can be both expensive and messy to fix. Also note that if there is a basement, you need to make sure that it doesn't show signs of flooding or water leakage from improper landscaping in the yard.

Defects in the Structure

When buying a home you're hoping to live in for an extended amount of time, you want to make sure that the structure is sound. You should keep an eye out for any damage to the foundation or flooring, as well as check that there isn't any water damage to ceilings or walls that could escalate to serious problems down the road. Some older homes may have cracking or settling in the foundation that's just a natural part of the aging process, but only a contractor or engineer can tell you the severity of those types of foundation issues. Don't let it put you off the sale if you're passionate about an older home, but be sure to do the proper follow up and research before proceeding.

Potential Roof Issues

Ideally a roof should not leak, have loose tiles or shingles, or be touching any tree branches. Roof repairs can become costly very quickly, and it's not like you can live in a house without a roof over your head! In addition to the dangers that trees and other debris pose in storms, they can also allow rodents access to your home or attic.

Improper Insulation

While in the attic or crawl space, take note of the condition of the insulation. Improper or missing insulation means that you'll be paying big-time energy bills in the winter. Insulation can also be a cozy place for unwanted roommates like rats or raccoons, and once they've made a home you may have to do a full or partial replacement of soiled insulation. (This is another item that I neglected in my own home inspection. The insulation was from the 1940s, but I thought it looked fine. It ended up being both very old and very expensive to replace!)

Broken Windows and Door Seals

If a door or window does not lay flush with the surrounding structure, you could be letting money slip through the cracks. Beyond that, broken seals on doors and windows can lead to water damage. This is typically a simple repair, but be sure to check for mold if you do find this issue during inspection.

Faulty Electrical Work

Depending on the age of the home, electrical outlets may be in short supply. This may not seem like an issue initially, but if there are exposed wires or extension cords running through the home then you should be on the lookout for potential electrical issues.

The Condition of the Plumbing

It's important to check the condition of all pipes, both for leaks and proper fit. Leaks in the plumbing inside the home can contribute to mold and other rot in floors and ceilings. You should also find out if the home is connected to a septic tank or public sewage.

Exterior Issues

Are there dimples or gaps in the siding? Do the gutters drain correctly? Fixing simple problems like these can help with the aesthetic appeal of the home and protect against issues such as water drainage.

So what happens when problems are discovered during the inspection? You can either ask the seller to fix them before closing, or ask to receive a credit at closing if the repairs are expensive or extensive. If you're negotiating with a bank on a foreclosure, you can ask them to give you a credit, but this rarely happens. You may have to decide if the home is worth the purchase price plus whatever amount you'll have to pay to fix the problem—or you can walk away.

Preparing for the Big Move

Since this is a book about preparing for homeownership and beyond, I'm including a section about what it costs to move households so that you and your budget can be fully prepared for the total homebuying experience. Here is a list of the budget-busting items to plan for when moving into your first home:

- Movers and/or a moving van or truck rental
- Money to turn on utilities: You'll have to pay a deposit if you're starting a new service or moving to a new city or state and can't transfer your existing services.
- Higher utility bills: If you're upgrading to a single family home, your utilities are going to increase because you are paying to run a larger home with more bells and whistles, as they say.
- Waste removal set up: The trash truck doesn't just magically appear at your house. (Whaaat?) You have to call and set it up and have the actual can and recycling bin delivered. (I know, what the hell, right?) You'll typically have to pay a deposit for this, too.
- Increased insurance premiums: Insuring a home is much more expensive than insuring your possessions in an apartment. You will have to provide proof of homeowners insurance to close on your mortgage, so you'll know prior to moving how much it will cost to insure your new home.

Other smaller items that you'll have to budget for when moving include:

- Condiments: These do not pack well, especially if you're moving in the warmer summer months. It's safer to buy them new after you move.
- Toilet bowl brushes: These also do not pack and travel well. (And also, gross.)
- Garbage cans: Unless it's a fancy upgraded model, opt for fresh, clean ones for your new home.
- Window coverings: Unless you negotiated with the seller to leave the coverings behind, you may be surprised by how many windows need to be covered and how expensive this can be.
- Lawn care tools.
- A minimal tool kit: This includes a screwdriver, hammer, pliers, etc.
- Shower curtain liners. I wouldn't pack these for the same reason that you wouldn't pack the toilet bowl brush.

I know I'm leaving out some basics like packing supplies, but you're already on top of that. I'm listing the things that you might have forgotten, and I want you to be as prepared as possible. Again, you're welcome.

A Few of the Surprises You'll Face as a Homeowner

When I worked at a hedge fund in New York City, we received ridiculously large Christmas bonuses. So large, in fact, that we joked about how we would start shopping for newer, bigger, apartments in January because of the yearly Christmas cash influx.

My colleague, Jen, who is now a famous author and still my favorite mentor and friend, thought the idea of owning a home was ridiculous. I was slowly warming to the idea of homeownership and she strongly discouraged against it.

"Lauren, houses have roofs that leak and heaters that break," she'd say. "You're too young to fool with that!"

"But renting is so expensive!" I countered.

"Yes, but it's because you're paying for the luxury of not having to worry about those things," she said.

I thought she was crazy at the time. How hard can it be to own a home? Well, it turns out she was right. Owning a home isn't difficult, but it requires you to reformat how you think after years of being a renter. For the first few months of owning my own place, I was so overwhelmed because it felt like there was always something to be fixed, monitored, and cared for... every single day.

Here is a list of items that you may have to start maintaining, or that may start eating into your budget, once you move into your first home.

Lawn Care

This may seem obvious to some, but I can promise you that when I bought my beautiful little home that sits on a half-acre lot, it never occurred to me that I just bought a beautiful little home...*on a half-acre lot.* While the home was under contract the same company that the real estate agency paid to mow the lawn while it was on the market kept coming to cut the grass and trim the hedges. So during the three month period from contract to close, the lawn was always immaculately maintained, and I never gave it a second thought.

I also closed on my home and moved in late fall, so the grass didn't grow during the colder months. But several months later, I walked onto my lawn and noticed that it was getting unruly. Like, really unruly. Oh dang, I have to mow the lawn, I thought. I know, so silly.

By pricing it out I found that it was (of course) cheaper to DIY than to pay for lawn care. My first trip to the hardware store yielded purchases of a lawn mower, hedge trimmers, and weed eater for the front walk. I'm glad I had months to recover from the home purchase, otherwise buying all of that lawn equipment would have really busted my budget.

Property Taxes

Property taxes are assessed by your city, and they're used to pay for things like street repair and schools. The amount of property tax that you will owe is based on the value of your home and the land it sits on. Depending on how developed your area is, property taxes can be very expensive.

Some lenders lump property taxes into the amount that you pay each month to your mortgage lender, or you may get an annual bill from your city. You can research how much you'll potentially owe by visiting your city auditor's website or by asking your mortgage broker for an estimate. Don't get blindsided by property taxes!

Air Filters

HVAC units have filters that need to be changed at least once every three months. (Something else I hadn't thought of.) Also, air filters come in very specific sizes, so be sure to write the specifications down before going to the store to purchase a new one. Otherwise you'll end up "eyeballing it" and having to go back to the store several times. (You know, just a helpful tip, I'm not speaking from experience or anything.)

Gutters

If you purchase a single-family home and live in a climate where the seasons change, leaves will likely get stuck in your gutters. If they get too full, water won't be able to drain properly when it rains—which can lead to leaks in your ceiling or other areas of your home. Many homeowners opt to break out the ladders and clear the gutters themselves, or you can hire a service to do it once or twice per year.

HOA Fees

If you live in a fancy condo or a neighborhood with shared amenities, you may have to pay a homeowners' association fee each month or on an annual basis. These fees help maintain facilities, such as a gym or pool, and usually cover trash removal and pest control, as well. An active homeowners' association is a good sign that your property is in a neighborhood where people care.

Some buildings calculate HOA fees based on square footage, while others may assess a flat monthly fee. This fee impacts your total monthly housing payment. For example, if you pay $900 for your mortgage and are required to pay an additional HOA fee of $300, then your total monthly payment is $1,200. So find out about any HOA fees up front to determine if your home is truly affordable.

Basic Repairs

Say you have a leak in your basement and don't know where it's coming from. When you rent, you can just call your landlord and have it taken care of. But when you own, you have to call a repairman, get on his schedule, and pay him for his work. This is where a healthy emergency fund really comes in handy.

Tips for Handling the Demands of Homeownership

Get Organized. Organize important papers like insurance policies, warranties, and appliance manuals in one place in your home. Be sure to keep a digital copy of your homeowners insurance policy in the cloud (or a hard copy in a safe deposit box, if you're super old school) in the event of a catastrophic home emergency like a fire, flood, or tornado.

Use an App. There are many smartphone applications that can help organize home information like paint colors, appliance model numbers, or the kind of air filter that your system takes. You can also keep this information in an Excel spreadsheet or a separate email file folder.

Buy Lightbulbs in Bulk. If you significantly upsize from an apartment to a larger condo or single family home, you will likely need to replace double the amount of bulbs. The owner before you won't put new bulbs in before departing, so make sure that you're prepared with a large quantity.

Three years later, the fact that I was so stressed over these maintenance issues seems like a distant memory. All of the small repairs and appointments now seem routine. I've had time to get used to them and selected vendors that I like working with year after year. Don't feel intimidated—it's all a learning curve.

I'll be honest, sometimes I do long for those days when it was my landlord's job to worry about home maintenance. But the positives of owning a home far outweigh the negatives, and at least with your own home you're helping to maintain its value. I promise, when it comes to loving and caring for a home, you'll get back everything that you put in.

CHAPTER 6

If You Want to Renovate

The biggest mistakes that I made when buying my first home can be easily summed up in two lessons. First, do not do a massive renovation as a first-time buyer. Second, vet your contractors very carefully.

In sharing my story, I've been able to talk with a lot of homeowners who decided to renovate. None of them have an amazing story where they've said, "I *loved* renovating, it was so easy and clean, and my contractor was amazing and didn't overcharge me. We finished on time and on budget!"

Yeah, most renovations are stressful. They're not like what you see on television. So why renovate at all, and how much does a renovation typically cost?

The answer is, it varies based on the work being done and prices in your area. But here's what I spent on my renovation:

- The total for the 203(k) renovation (more on this later) and overages was about $58,000.
- I have spent about $6,800 since 2013, which brings my grand total to $64,800.

I was able to renovate most of my house for that amount. I didn't knock down walls, but I did have to re-plumb, re-wire, and re-HVAC the entire house, which made my renovation particularly complicated.

When the process began, the truth is, my ex-fiancé and I loved our contractor. He seemed humble and kind. But soon we started getting the sneaking suspicion that he was taking money off the top because every single project ended up going over budget. Overages are a part of any project—but every time? Come on.

For example, he'd install a fixture and then say that he needed additional money for an extra part that "wasn't included." He'd quote a price to refinish the floors and then after they were finished, he'd say that it would cost extra to reinstall the trim and molding around the floor. Typically, this is included; or if it isn't, a good contractor communicates up front what the charges are going to be. Something similar happened with the kitchen cabinets; they came without knobs and he told me knobs would be extra. I went to Home Depot and took care of that one myself. Imagine six months of always being told that a project needs more money!

Things came to a head when it came time for inspections and the house failed to pass—which is a sure sign of sloppy work. My contractor was constantly having to redo projects in order to meet code specifications and get a passing certificate. One of our last inspections was for the new HVAC. His workers had put the new unit on the existing concrete pad, but more recent building codes stipulated that it couldn't be located so close to the house next door. In order to be compliant, a new slab would have to be poured on the other side of the house and all of the electrical would have to be re-routed.

The cost to re-run the HVAC? $3,500. That's $3,500 on a project that was *already* $5,000 over budget (including the 10% contingency fund we blew through). The contractor said that I should pay for it. I said that it wasn't my job to know the new building codes—wasn't that what I was paying him for? We were at a standstill, and weeks went by without the HVAC getting fixed. We couldn't move forward with the second inspection because he and I refused to talk to one another and come to a resolution. In my defense, my fiancé and I had also broken up and he moved out while this was happening, so my mind and emotional bandwidth were at max capacity.

The final renovation check from the bank came early (this was part of the 203(k) renovation loan process, which I'll detail later). The way it worked was that once the bank cut the check from my 203(k) loan fund, they'd mail it to me, and then I'd endorse it and hand it over to my contractor.

The payments had gone smoothly up until that point, but I didn't feel comfortable handing over the final payment while we still had the HVAC inspection outstanding. Let's just say that after I told him he wasn't getting the check, things got ugly. He came by my house with his workers, and he threatened me via text and email. Even though I was clear that he wasn't getting the money until we resolved the HVAC issue, he wouldn't leave me alone.

Between the renovations and breaking off the engagement, I was emotionally drained. My parents intervened with their attorney, who advised me that it would be faster, easier, and cheaper to pay the contractor with the final check and give him the additional $3,500 to finish the work. Even though it stung to pay him when I felt like I was in the right, that's what I did—and I made the right choice. I'm not sure if I could have dealt with the stress from that situation much longer.

His horrible work cost me the 203(k) renovation loan, all of my savings, and additional money that I had to borrow from my parents. In the four years since then, I've rebuilt my savings, paid my parents back, and paid off all of my credit card debt, but the stress of the entire renovation still lingers in my mind.

I don't want one young gal's horror story to deter you from buying a fixer-upper if that's what your heart desires, but it's important to go into the project with your eyes open. So, for all of you who want to renovate in order to create a home that feels like yours, update an older home (those guys need love too), or create equity in your investment, the rest of this chapter is for you.

The biggest silver lining of my experience is that I got a crash course in rehabbing properties, and I'm about to share that knowledge with you.

How to Pay for Your Renovation

Here are the four ways that homeowners typically pay for home renovations:

1. Save their pennies and fund the renovation in cash—or put it on a credit card—and do each project piece by piece.
2. Use a home equity line of credit (HELOC) once they've been in the home for a certain amount of time and after they've built enough equity that can be used to finance upgrades.
3. A personal loan from a bank.
4. A 203(k) renovation loan.

If you're looking to buy a home and want to begin work before or shortly after moving in, a 203(k) renovation loan may be a good fit for you. Many millennials opt to go this route because they often don't have enough cash on hand to purchase a home and also invest in renovations.

What Is a 203(k) Renovation Loan?

Basically, a 203(k) renovation loan allows you to borrow money for a home renovation at the same time that you are borrowing money for a mortgage. The 203(k) product lumps both the mortgage and renovation loan funds together into one monthly payment.

There are two different types of 203(k) renovation loans, and they are the Standard 203(k) loan, and the Streamlined 203(k) loan.

The Standard 203(k) loan is used for more extensive projects like total remodels, structural work, etc., where the amount borrowed will be greater than $35,000.

The Streamlined 203(k) is used for more cosmetic-type projects like countertops, flooring, and paint, where the amount borrowed will be less than $35,000.

I used the Standard 203(k) loan for my renovation because I needed more than $35,000 to make my home livable.

Using my own purchase as an example, when I first applied for a mortgage I was qualified for up to $130,000 as a single woman earning an annual salary of $40,000. I could either go with a traditional mortgage and buy a move-in ready home for $130,000, or, if I wanted to buy a fixer-upper and borrow bank money to renovate it, I'd need to buy a home for less and factor in the amount that

I would need to borrow—while keeping in mind that $130,000 maximum amount.

So I bought a home for $65,000 and borrowed $58,000 to renovate it, for a total investment of $123,000. Nice and tidy and under my maximum budget!

Each month that I make my mortgage payment, I'm paying off an amount that includes both the mortgage plus the money that I borrowed to renovate my home. There's no discernible difference in my account between mortgage and renovation loan money; it's all just one lump sum.

How to Use a 203(k) Renovation Loan

The 203(k) renovation loan required me to pay out-of-pocket for an FHA consultant, or someone to oversee and make sure the work on my home was getting done. This prevents fraud. Neither the consultant nor I had direct access to the money the way that we would through a HELOC.

Upon closing, the money for the renovations was delivered into an escrow account, and I had my own specialist at Wells Fargo overseeing the money. We, meaning me, the bank, and my contractor, had four pre-determined check-in and payout dates. By each date, my contractor was supposed to have finished certain projects.

The 203(k) consultant would come to my home and inspect the work at each check-in point, and then send a report to Wells Fargo. My specialist at the bank would verify with me via email that the information in the report was correct. If everything checked out, my specialist cut a check from the account, made out to my contractor, for one-fourth the amount of the whole project.

The check would get overnighted for me to sign and give to my contractor, but I never had control of the money or access to it directly. So you can see from the process that there are checks and balances in place to make sure that funds do not get misused.

The Benefits of Using a 203(k) Renovation Loan

Many millennials have a hard time swinging the down payment, much less the thousands of dollars for a renovation job, but the 203(k) renovation loan makes both possible. I also liked being able to have the home exactly the way I wanted, which made my first foray into homeownership even sweeter. You never get exactly what you want in a rental!

There are also stipulations and timeliness clauses built into the loan. If the contractor wants to be paid, work has to begin within thirty days of closing and be completed within six months.

From a financial perspective, because the renovation loan is lumped together with the mortgage, you're still able to borrow at a low interest rate. In fact, the $58,000 that I borrowed from the bank was at the same interest rate as my mortgage—a super low 3.25%.

There is a darker side to the 203(k) renovation loan, however, that I haven't mentioned. Because of all the paperwork and communication involved regarding payment and inspection dates, you have to start and end the project with the same contractor. If you disagree with your contractor or don't like his work—which is what happened to me—this can create multiple issues.

Also, because the project amount is set in advance based on that contractor's bid, it is to the contractor's benefit to do cheap work so he can pocket larger margins—also what happened to me. Contractors I've worked with since then have estimated that I paid $58,000 for about $40,000 worth of work.

There are very few avenues of recourse if something does go wrong with a 203(k) renovation loan, and trust me, I looked. The options are either to stop the work and fight it out with your contractor, the consultant, and the bank; or keep moving forward and try to get your money back later. From my experience, this was the biggest drawback to using a 203(k) renovation loan, and it can make it difficult to find quality contractors to work with.

Having access to such a large amount of money up front may lead millennials to borrow more than they can afford in an attempt to make their homes look Instagram-perfect. Be sure that your home is still at a price point that your monthly budget can comfortably afford when accounting for your mortgage and renovation loan.

How to Get the Most Bang for Your Buck

I think "renovation reluctance" is a good thing. In interviews that I give and articles that I write for the press, I often recommend that first-time buyers forgo large-scale renovation projects. Why? There's too much of a learning curve with first-time homeownership as it is; do not make it even more stressful by throwing in unknown projects that cost thousands of dollars.

But then again, buying a fixer-upper can turn out to be a great financial move and yield big returns down the road when you want to sell. If you choose to do renovations on a home that you won't live in for the long term, either for comfort or for investment purposes, it's important to be strategic with your projects so that you can get the biggest return when you sell and move into your forever home.

When thinking of potential upgrades, it's important to consider if the costs will outweigh the benefits. You should also make decisions based on your budget, time constraints, and the type of home that you're renovating. A modern kitchen can look out of place in a historic home, just as wood paneling looks dated in a newer, more updated home. I'm surprised how many people forget these simple rules when doing their renovation projects!

The projects below can be adapted to many different styles and budgets, making them a good starting point for those looking to renovate and spend smartly.

Replacing or Remodeling the Entry Door

According to *Remodeling Magazine's* 2015 Cost vs. Value Report, the national average return on investment for replacing an entry door with a new steel door is 101.8%—meaning that you could potentially make money off replacing your front door!

There are many options for door renovations as well, including low-cost DIY projects such as adding a fresh coat of paint, installing address numbers, or replacing hardware, which increases value with less out-of-pocket expense.

Insulating the Attic

On average, an insulated attic recoups 116.9% of its investment; it's fairly inexpensive (think less than $2,000, including materials); and can help save money on energy bills. A triple win!

Adding an Attic Bedroom

Creating an attic bedroom increases a home's value by an average of $39,908, mainly because of the additional square footage. Just keep in mind that costs for this project can add up quickly. You'll need to strengthen the floors, have stair access, and add a window in order for the room to count as an additional bedroom in your home.

Remodeling the Kitchen

A kitchen remodel is consistently at the top of the most desired renovation projects, and having an updated kitchen will increase your resale value while making a big impression on buyers. It may not increase your value dollar-for-dollar, but kitchens and bathrooms are generally sound investments.

Replacing the Siding

This is a great option for those that feel satisfied with a home's interior but are looking for a major appearance change. Of all the siding options available, fiber cement and vinyl siding have the highest return on investment, according to the 2015 Cost vs. Value Report.

How to Save Money on Renovations

Just because you're a first-time homeowner doesn't mean that you have to make the same mistakes that I did. Here are a few of my favorite tips for saving money on renovation projects.

Do Your Own Demo and Cleanup

If you don't have to pay your contractor's crew to do demolition and cleanup, you can save yourself a lot of billable hours. Even though it's often dirty, back-breaking work, it's not a skilled job—literally anyone can do it. By doing your own demo you'll save money, and as a bonus you'll feel like you're contributing to the beautification of your home.

Salvage What You Can

It may make sense to completely redo a room in your home, but if there are things about it that you love—the vintage cabinets or trim, for example—maybe all it needs is a fresh coat of paint. By salvaging what you can, you'll save small amounts here and there, which can really add up over time.

Kitchen remodels in particular are costly. Go into the project with an idea of what you're looking to replace entirely and what you're planning to repurpose. If you're planning to purchase new appliances and need more room in your budget, consider lower-cost options for other projects, such as resurfacing countertops or refinishing and replacing knobs on cabinets.

Keep the Floor Plan the Same

I know the trend these days is a super-open floor plan, but if you can get away with remodeling a kitchen or bathroom and not moving the plumbing to a different area in the room, you will potentially save thousands of dollars.

Pick Up Your Own Supplies

Contractors and retailers will charge you for pick-up and delivery. If you have access to a truck, use it to save yourself money on delivery fees.

Shop Clearance and Secondhand

You know the old cliché, "One man's trash is another man's treasure?" I have never found this to be truer than when shopping for appliances, light fixtures, and hardware. Craigslist, antique stores, eBay, and other secondhand sites offer downright exquisite deals on lighting, furniture, cabinets, flooring, and hardware fixtures.

My motto is to never pay full price—and it's saved me a bundle on the decorative details of my home.

How to Find a Good Contractor

Returning to my own renovation story, the biggest mistake that I made was in not vetting my contractor properly. You may cringe while reading this next sentence: I only interviewed the one contractor and only received one bid. The contractor I used (yes, the same one that screwed me over) was a referral from my real estate agent and I trusted her opinion. I didn't even think to check his references.

Because I was using the 203(k) renovation loan, I have to admit that my renovation budget felt a bit like "play money" because it wasn't cash coming out of my hand. The bottom line is that I didn't take the whole process as seriously as I should have. This was the most expensive purchase of my life, so why wasn't I paying more attention?

I cannot express enough how important it is to truly get to know the people that you're working with on your first home purchase.

Get Referrals From People You Trust

In hindsight, getting a recommendation from my real estate agent wasn't the best move. I liked working with her, but my contractor had never done renovation work for her; she just knew him through church.

This is why I recommend asking friends, family, and people that you trust for referrals. We shouldn't play around when it comes to this kind of cash! If you don't know anyone who has recently renovated her home, search reputable sources like Angie's List for referrals in your area, and then proceed to the next steps on this list.

Interview Contractors Before Getting Bids

Whether you receive a referral or find a contractor through an online search, you should thoroughly interview each potential contractor by phone before meeting and getting a bid for your project. Here are a few questions to ask during the interview:

- How many other projects will you be working on at the same time?
- Are you licensed, bonded, and insured? (If not—run far, far away!)
- Will subcontractors complete any of the work and, if so, which projects will be subcontracted?

- How long have you worked with your subcontractors?
- Will you be working at the property every day?
- Is your preferred method of communication phone, text, or email?
- What are your favorite types of projects to work on?

Ask for References—and Check Them!

Close out every interview by asking for the contractor's references. Call each name provided and ask about their experience working with said contractor. What did they like? What didn't they like? What did they find frustrating? You may have to specifically ask if they had any complaints, as most people—especially a reference—probably won't mention it unless directly asked.

Checking references is the most crucial part of the contractor hiring process because it's the only chance you'll have to engage in an honest conversation about your potential contractor's work ethic.

Know Exactly What Kind of Project You Want

It's expected that you'll add on another project here and there as renovations get under way, but it's better for your budget and your relationship with your contractor if you try to come up with an exhaustive list of what you'd like to have done before the renovation begins.

Sign a Detailed Agreement

At a minimum, you should draft an agreement that outlines the scope of the project, how much it will cost, when payment is expected, and when work will be completed.

Make Sure Your Contractor Gets the Appropriate Permits

Don't let your contractor skip on the permits. Sure, it's possible that you could get away with using a contractor that's not licensed, but if you get caught you could end up paying hefty fines to the city and face delays that will eat into your budget and timeline.

Final Money Tips for Renovators

Here are a few tips to keep both your personal finances and renovation budget on track during a big, multi-week home renovation.

Have a Contingency Fund

Most contractors will include a 5% to 10% contingency fund in their initial project bid. This amount is added to the budget to cover any overages or unforeseen costs. If your bid doesn't include a contingency fund, ask your contractor how overages will be handled and plan for it in your personal budget.

Don't Pay More Than 10% Up Front

The amount of deposit needed to begin work should be outlined in your detailed agreement, but I don't recommend paying more than 10% of the project total. This should be plenty to get your contractor the supplies and crew necessary to get started. With a 203(k) renovation loan, you're not allowed to pay the contractor a deposit, as he can be paid only for work completed.

Keep Communication Open

Obviously, I didn't handle the situation with my contractor correctly. The time that I spent too upset to deal with him cost me money and weeks on my renovation timeline.

I realize now that it's important for your financial wellbeing to keep the lines of communication as open as possible. Whether the money for the project is on credit, in your savings account, or from a 203(k) escrow fund, it's your money and you are responsible for it.

You're entitled to ask as many questions as you want and do as many check-ins as you please. (Repeat that to yourself every day if you have to!)

The Positive Side of Renovating a Home

I'm not going to lie—I'm the poster child for how much money you can make renovating a property. Even with the ups and downs, it was well worth it in the end. Since I bought my home I've earned:

- $40,000 in a state income-tax credit that I applied for and received for rehabbing an historic property in the state of Georgia.
- $3,000 each year in loan forgiveness for living in my home as a primary residence. This is part of the down payment assistance program that I leveraged to get into the home for $1,800, which I wrote about in Chapter Two.
- $16,410 from renting out bedrooms over the last three years.
- $60,000 increase in home equity.

In total I've earned $119,410 on my home, which breaks down to $39,803 per year as of the time this book goes to press. I mean, $40,000 each year just to live in my home...isn't that insane?

I count my ability to make money on my home—even after all the mistakes that I made—on the fact that I picked a property primed for growth. When I think about how I could have been renting this entire time instead of having my money *making money*, I know that I did the right thing, despite all of the trouble along the way.

Renovating isn't all bad, but make no mistake, it isn't for the faint of heart.

CONCLUSION

———•———

I often like to joke that the first year of homeownership is similar to—what I assume to be—the first year of marriage. The first year is often the most difficult because you don't know what to expect. You're learning as you go and constantly changing your expectations. You're used to something different, and although your new life is just as great as you imagined it to be, it often involves a lot of hard work.

I've never regretted buying my home. After all, it's turned out to be the best investment that I've ever made. But if I had to do it all over again, here is what I would have done differently during that first year:

I Would Have Prioritized Renovations Like an Investor

It's an old real estate adage that kitchens are what sell the home and bathrooms hold their value. Thinking that I was making a long-term home for a family, I took on renovation projects for my comfort that I knew might not hold their value when I sell. I wish that I had prioritized the renovation projects through the precise eye of an investor looking to make money.

I Would Have Asked More Questions

I think that being young and naive I expected some-one—anyone—to come charging in and ask the important questions for me, not remembering that the biggest part of being an adult is initiating the tough conversations on my own.

I Would Have Done More Research

There were some periods during the homebuying process where I felt like I did the proper research and it benefited me. But there were other times when I wish that I had done more. For example:

- I only obtained quotes from two lenders when shopping for my mortgage.
- I received a single bid for the renovation work that I had done.
- I didn't check my contractor's references. I just got a "good vibe" and trusted my gut. (It turns out that I should have backed up my gut feeling with a little hard research.)

I Would Have Budgeted More

I had a budget for the home purchase and renovation, but even with the down payment assistance that I received from the city of Atlanta, I barely had any room for overages. If I had done more research on the cost of home-related items, I would have been able to make a better budget.

....

My new rule of thumb? Whenever I estimate what something home-related is going to cost, I double it...just in case. It's better to be surprised than stressed.

....

The Positive Side of Being a Homeowner

In closing this book, I'd be remiss if I didn't highlight a few of the wonderful splendors that have come with owning my own home.

Greater Financial Stability

As millennials, our decision to become homeowners will pay off down the road. By the time our late 30s and 40s come around, we'll have significant equity in our homes or we'll have potentially sold them for a nice profit.

Equity to Use Down the Line

If you stay in your home for a spell, you'll build equity which can be leveraged for future investments like grad school, a business, your child's college, or debt payoff.

Passive Income

Owning my own home has allowed me to rent out one of my bedrooms to recoup renovation costs and reduce the burden of my monthly mortgage. Having that extra income, especially after I left my full-time job to build my own business, was a life saver.

Rental income has hands down been the nicest, shiniest silver lining of my homebuying journey. I know that renting isn't feasible for everyone, but all homeowners can Airbnb their pad for extra cash when they're out of town. Think about new ways to leverage your asset to make more money!

Empowerment

And finally, although it's completely cheesy and cliché to say, buying a home makes you feel like a baller. You *own* something now, and you had the intelligence, wherewithal, and good credit history to make it happen. Something just feels different once you own a place; the holidays are different, gatherings are different—it all feels warmer and more permanent.

I know that I've provided a gritty, honest look at homeownership, but it's also a beautiful, wonderful thing, too—and don't let anyone tell you otherwise.

ABOUT THE AUTHOR

L auren Bowling is the award-winning blogger and editor behind FinancialBestLife.com (formerly *L Bee and the Money Tree*). Blogging since 2012, Lauren is now a recognized thought leader on millennial finance and first-time homeownership. Her expertise has been featured in the pages of *Redbook* and *Woman's Day* magazines and on leading online financial news sites including *Forbes*, *The Huffington Post*, *CNNMoney* and *U.S. News and World Report*. Lauren happily resides in Atlanta, Georgia.

INDEX

CPSIA information can be obtained
at www.ICGtesting.com
Printed in the USA
LVHW082335270519
619236LV00028B/502/P